# THE
# LOW
# PASSIONS

## ALSO BY ANDERS CARLSON-WEE

*Dynamite*
*Mercy Songs* (with Kai Carlson-Wee)
*Two-Headed Boy* (with Kai Carlson-Wee)

# THE
# LOW
# PASSIONS

**POEMS**     **ANDERS CARLSON-WEE**

W. W. NORTON & COMPANY

INDEPENDENT PUBLISHERS SINCE 1923

NEW YORK | LONDON

Copyright © 2019 by Anders Carlson-Wee

All rights reserved
Printed in the United States of America
First Edition

For information about permission to reproduce selections from this book,
write to Permissions, W. W. Norton & Company, Inc.,
500 Fifth Avenue, New York, NY 10110

For information about special discounts for bulk purchases, please contact
W. W. Norton Special Sales at specialsales@wwnorton.com or 800-233-4830

Manufacturing by Lake Book Manufacturing, Inc.
Book design by Mary Austin Speaker
Production manager: Beth Steidle

Library of Congress Cataloging-in-Publication Data

Names: Carlson-Wee, Anders, author.
Title: The low passions : poems / Anders Carlson-Wee.
Description: First edition. | New York : W. W. Norton & Company,
[2019] | Includes bibliographical references.
Identifiers: LCCN 2018046579 | ISBN 9780393652383 (hardcover)
Classification: LCC PS3603.A7534 L69 2019 | DDC 811/.6—dc23
LC record available at https://lccn.loc.gov/2018046579

W. W. Norton & Company, Inc., 500 Fifth Avenue, New York, N.Y. 10110
www.wwnorton.com

W. W. Norton & Company Ltd., 15 Carlisle Street, London W1D 3BS

2 3 4 5 6 7 8 9 0

*for Mom, Dad, Kai, and Olaf*


*for all those who took me in when I was far from home*


*and in loving memory of Scott Christopher Maxwell*

# CONTENTS

# THE
# LOW
# PASSIONS

## RIDING THE OWL'S EYE

Out of all the dumpsters that could have been
empty, all the weather that could have bloomed
over the prairie and ruined me, all the cars
that could have sped by without hesitating and left me
on the fog line nameless forever. The trains
that could have taken my legs. The men
that could have pulled a switchblade and opened me
like a flood enfolding the red North Dakota clay.
Out of all the hazards we pass through
in amazement, all the stories we tell of luck
and good fortune and prayer and survival, it is always
our own lungs that dry up and darken,
our own miles that straighten, our own hunger
that wanes. The Lord gives us mountains
and we fail to mine out that grandness.
The Lord gives us trains and we waste those distances
transporting coal. Some say the world is broken,
some say the Good Lord has forsaken our dreams,
but I say it is our own throat that grows
the cancer, our own asthma that blackens our breath
to a wheeze. And the truth is, the mile-long train
will always crawl past. The socket-fixed gaze
of the owl's skull will always turn perfectly
backwards. We will always be bodies among ghosts.
And what is important to them is not how we ride

on the westbound freighter, not how we shiver,
not how we crawl crooked and thin
and climb yet again into the trembling eyehole.
It is not about suffering. It is not about fear.
We must peer out from inside the owl's eye.
Watch the coal dust cook in the wind eddies.
Watch it linger. Watch it spiral thinly as it bruises
the blue-faded mind of the buffalo sky.
We must be the pupil that swells in the coming darkness.
The cargo worth carrying across the distances.

# COUNTY 19

I twist in my seat beside the woman who picked me up
on County 19, reaching back to help her son
eat his Happy Meal. I fly a french fry through the air,
thinking how weird it is to hitch a ride on the road
I've driven so many times with my dad—
the route between our house and the old folks home
where Grandma lasted alone for fourteen years.
Each time we visited: the veins wider, bluer,
the ankles thinner, the distances between bedsores
diminished, the cheer my dad convinced himself to feel
as he repeated the litany: *I am your son.*
*This is your grandson. We're so happy to see you.*
The woman asks me where I'm going
and I say as far as you can take me,
but as we pass the old folks home I tell her to pull over.
The boy is finished with his Happy Meal and now
he points at the bruise on his elbow and says *Ouch.*
His mom nods at him in the rearview as I get out.
*That's right*, she says. *Ouch.* There is the low roofline,
the sign with a bible quote in changeable letters,
my grandma's old window as blank as it was
when she lived here, some earth dug up
in the bordering cornfield for construction
of a new wing. I think about barging through the doors
and demanding to see Elizabeth Wee, making

some kind of scene. I think about setting up camp
in the hole in the cornfield and refusing to leave.
But instead I wander the grounds for a while.
I lie in the parking lot's grass island and watch
cornstalks feathering the road with lank shadows,
the sunlight dipping down into the tassels.
I want speed. I want new people. To ditch
this slow sanitary drain of golden light,
my pastor parents and their immovable faith,
this town's brown river exhausting its banks.
Elizabeth is underground. So is my cousin.
Stones like polished teeth in the family plot.
In the twilight I walk back to the shoulder
and catch a ride from a farmer hauling a trailer
stacked with hay bales three-high. When he asks me
where I'm going I say as far as you can take me.

## DYNAMITE

My brother hits me hard with a stick
so I whip a choke chain

across his face. We're playing
a game called *Dynamite*

where everything you throw
is a stick of dynamite,

unless it's pine. Pine sticks
are rifles and pinecones are grenades,

but everything else is dynamite.
I run down the driveway

and back behind the garage
where we keep the leopard frogs

in buckets of water
with logs and rock islands.

When he comes around the corner
the blood is pouring

out of his nose and down his neck
and he has a hammer in his hand.

I pick up his favorite frog
and say If you come any closer

I'll squeeze. He tells me I won't.
He starts coming closer.

I say a hammer isn't dynamite.
He reminds me that everything is dynamite.

## FINDING JOSH

Seven Camels touching on the bedstand
in a measured row, like a pan flute

with flush pipes that, when blown,
all hit one note. An eighth, unlit,

fits loosely in his curled fingers.
A few empty Coors rim the bathroom sink,

pull tabs removed. There's no need
to check for a pulse, hold a credit card

for breath. I've worked with carcasses
the size of men. Gagged at the odor of a doe

letting go, smoked flies off piles of organs,
heard the wet rip of skin teased free

in oval sheets. I know the creature
is no longer there. No longer anywhere.

But the hair still spins the cowlick.
The neck still cranes as if to listen.

## GREAT PLAINS FOOD BANK

The wind is in the trees again, and I'm thinking it's a wonder
the body can move. The way the mother at the Fargo food bank
fingers a can of concentrated juice. The way the line keeps
heaving forward. The way the child tugs the heavy skirt.
My job is to look for the elderly, help them load. Like the guy
who grew up in Oslo and is still trying to make it to Bergen.
It's a straight shot on the train, he says, but you have to be
in Norway to catch it. I lift his meat and yogurt onto a cart.
I wait as he chooses nine of the least bruised carrots.
The trunk of his car has the smell of dried flowers, and his
baguettes fit lengthwise easily. But before I help him lower
himself into the driver's seat, and before his hands pass over
one another, turning into the northbound traffic, he tells me
I'm young. Tells me it's spring. Says I should be out of here,
heading for Bergen. I know he's right. I know he's
so goddamn right. I stand as still as I can as he leaves.

# LEAVING FARGO

We crammed in McAlpine's Pulse and drove
west out of Fargo to see the train wreck.
Late summer and the heat moaning
from the radiator, smoke gushing from the seams
in the hood, all of us snake-biting
McAlpine's neck when he admitted
he'd thinned the coolant to try to make it
stretch. We passed Whale-O-Wash
where the volleyball girls held up cardboard
signs, did barefoot high kicks in bikinis,
offering five-dollar specials to raise funds
for their team. We passed M&H Gas.
Ironclad. Rickert's Bar. The Hardee's parking lot
where the Moorhead kids lounged on the hoods
of their cars, but we didn't flick them off
because we knew about Garcia,
who'd just hung himself in his father's closet
with a belt. Skateland. Hebron Brick.
My mother's church on Division boarded up
and watermarked at the windows, signed
by the height of the flood in the spring.
Indian Triumph. Curt's Lock and Key.
Ameristeel where McApline worked
with his uncle on weekends. The bums asleep
on layers of newspaper in the bushes

beside Bell State Bank. Tintmasters. Dakota
Electric. The rubble and brick where last winter
a lady carved a swastika into her wrist
before burning down her own fortuneteller business.
The old folks home where wheelchaired vets
waved out the windows at whoever
came by. Bozak flicked them off
and we all laughed. We passed the last trees
on the edge of town and gunned down
a county road through the ripening beets,
cranking up the windows and blasting the heat
as McAlpine pushed the Pulse above 90.
We called this Operation Desert Storm—
the North Dakota roads so flat and straight
you could hit 95 before the car started to quiver,
McAlpine screaming into the windshield:
*Oppy Desy! Oppy Desy!* All of us peeling
off our shirts and wearing them like turbans.
As we hit 99 I dug a onesy from the glovebox
and packed it and held it to McAlpine's
trembling lips. *This one's for Garcia*, he said.
We passed 100. Out in the fields the heat-
lifted kinks of cargo came into view.
It was the wreck we were looking for—
a junker from Wolf Point, Williston, Minot,
Grand Forks. A local. Low priority. Loaded
with hoppers, tankers, Canadian grainers,

gondolas hauling scrap metal to Duluth.
Somehow the clay and rain had fucked up
the rails and caused the freight to buckle
at the couplers, but nobody had died.
The conductor and his crew rolled on down the line,
drifting in the engine unit, watching
in the rearview as the mile-long train turtled
into the sugar beets and began to pile.

# BIRDCALLS

I crept around the dark train yard
while my brother watched for bulls.
Two days deep into the Badlands
and all our water gone. We had a birdcall
for if you saw something and another
for if you heard. A silent yard eight strings wide
with a few junkers parked. The horizon
a dull burn. The rails lit dimly by dew.
I was looking for the water bottles
the conductors used and threw out the windows
with maybe a sip left inside them.
I found one by stepping on it.
I sucked it like a leech. I stumbled
up and down the ballast and found five more,
unbuttoning my shirt and nesting them
against my chest upright and capless.
We had the sandpiper for if you should run
and the flycatcher for if you should hide.
I can't remember why we had the loon.
I crouched in the space between coal trains,
cradling the bottles and feeling the weight
of how little I had to spill.
I rubbed coal on my face. I felt crazy.
I thought about being found like this.
I tried to imagine what my story would be.

A version with my brother in it.
A version with no brother. I swear
I could smell rain a thousand miles away.
I could smell rain in the soot. I folded my hands
around my lips and made the gray ghost,
which told him where I was.
And also meant stay alert.
And also meant some other things
only owls understood.

## LIVING

I get everything I need for free.
These boots came from the factory
dumpster on the far side of town. This hat
was moldering on the kitchen floor
in the foreclosed home I picked through.
This coat, this backpack, this brand-
name headlamp. I got this cornmeal
behind the grocery store, this flatbread
behind the bakery, this french press
in the alleyway next to the coffee shop in uptown.
This bible in a bum camp, this banjo
in a trashcan, this headless mannequin
in a free pile outside Honest Ed's Antiques.
The British call it skipping.
The Brazilians call it living, call it vida.
*Vida que surgi de nada.* Life out of nothing.
I bike past the butcher's on Pike
and find a bag full of pigs.
None of them whole. A few sets of hooves,
a half torso, two heads, another head
with no nose, a leg, a pile of coiled tails
slowly uncoiling like white worms
taken out of a hole. Most of it going
musty, the muscle falling away
from the fascia, the skin drained of color

and feeling like withered pumpkin.
But some of it might be good.
A pair of milky gloves is clumped up
and tangled among the little hairless tails.
I dig them out. I blow to check
for holes. I begin sorting the pigs.

## ICEFISHER

The man sets the fish house far out
on the lake. Drills the hole.
Scoops the slush out with a ladle.
Silence and the lake and the man.
The pine hills folded in fog,
faded to ash and gunpowder.
The maple leaves fallen and lost
in the snow. The gray ghost
thin and sinewy, moving off through
the coal-black remnants of branches.
If you cannot see it in winter
you will never see it.
The man goes into the dark house
and lowers his lure. The deep hole
glows. The water is clear.
The low hoot of the owl simmers
the shore meridian as evening
comes on and the hole
darkens. He breathes into his hands.
He lets out a little more line.

## MCDONALD'S

You walk all night and into the next day
to survive the sudden October snow.

You have no money or hope of money.
Your backpack is a cloth sack with duct-

tape straps and safety pins in place
of zippers. Your gloves have no thumbs,

just holes, just unraveling half fingers.
You've come inside for the heat,

for plastic spoons, mayo, salt and sugar
packets, hand napkins you'll ball later

for insulation beneath your clothes.
You've come for the bathroom—soap

to scrub your face, your neck, your pits,
toilet rolls for kindling flames as you camp

alone tonight in the woods or in a silo.
Mirror for popping your zits, hand dryer

for drying your hair, your musty coat.
You've come to run warm water

over hands you can no longer feel,
come to sit and rest and do nothing,

and think nothing, and be no one.
You ask the boy at the counter

if you can have some water. He nods,
tapping his foot to a bluegrass tune,

slides a paper cup toward you
with a smooth hand, asks

out of habit if that will be everything.

## PRIMER

And what if you have nothing?
I pick up a stick. Yes, that's always first.
And next? I see what I can see around me.
Find the sun or moon. Find high ground.
Find north by where the moss grows.
Yes. Now close your eyes. Find them.
The sun's behind. I can feel it
on my neck. High ground's to my right.
North's ahead. Yes. And the wind?
The wind's west. It cools my left temple.
Yes. And next? If I can bug out
I bug out. Otherwise I go high
and dig a foxhole and tie something bright
above me. You're forgetting something.
Right—first I cut my name in the dirt,
then I go high. Yes. And next?
I walk a loop with my bright thing in sight.
If I find a better stick I switch for it.
Yes. And if you need to cry?
I crawl inside my foxhole and cry.
And what do you tell yourself as you cry?
Someone's coming. Yes. And what if
no one comes? Each hour I call
in all directions. I listen. Yes.
And what do you listen for?

Sounds that shouldn't be there. Yes.
Sounds that should be there but aren't.
Yes. And what have you heard
since we started? A bird. Yes. Another bird
far away. Yes. A gust in the trees.
Yes. Your voice, if your voice counts.
Yes, my voice counts.

# THE MUSCLES IN THEIR THROATS

The Neanderthals tracked mammoths through the snow.
Postholed twice between each of the creature's
blue-hued prints. Peered down at the toe digs, hoping
for any fissures in the powder that might be a sign
of weakness. Nightmares larger than the caves
they slept in. Before they hunted them, they fire-hardened
their spears, but as they bored holes in the midriff
and carted home great slabs of marbled meat, and later,
as they boiled the pelvis for a red-marrow broth,
we don't know for certain how much they could say
to each other. It's no different now. My brother
strips boughs off the wind-stunted pines at tree line
and stacks them on a boulder. I drag them over scree
to the A-frame we're building on the shore of a nameless
alpine lake. We need the branches for insulation.
A foot thick for every ten degrees below sixty.
This high up, it's bound to freeze. We know the spearheads
were basically the same for two hundred thousand years.
And the design worked, though the hunters
had to get feverishly close—the bones we've studied
are riddled with burst fractures, the skulls
remolded from concussions. I squeeze inside
to see where the light is breaking through.
In the cold I watch my breath escaping out the holes.
But when I try to tell my brother where to add

more boughs, he darkens what's already dark enough.
The horseshoe-shaped muscles in their throats
were anatomically modern, so there's no real reason
they wouldn't have been able to speak. When scientists
finish a life-size model of the esophagus, we'll finally hear
what their voices must have sounded like.

# LODESTAR

Nothing you'll find more orphan than the heart.
The dim mission of its reptile-eyed insomnia,
its nameless drive, its bulging catalytic beat.
The night sky wheels with the same fever, as if thrown
from a bowler's hand with english on it. Orion.
Ursa Minor. You cannot constellate desire any more
than you can braid cord from the tongue's sinewed utterance
of a name, a name hallowed at night into the wind,
the wind tethered to the earth like flame to black spruce,
quartered and four years dried. Beargrass. Monk's Hood Lichen.
Methuselah's Beard. Old Man on the Mountain.
You take your bearings by a belt of pulsing stars.
You turn to reckon with the one that doesn't move.
Polaris. Dog's Tail. Leiðarstjarna. Nail. Mismar.

## GATHERING FIREWOOD ON TINPAN

I bundle them against my chest, not sure
if they're dry enough. Gauging how long
they'll keep me warm by the thickness.
I step around carefully, looking for
the deadest, searching the low places
for something small and old that will catch.
I pick up the dander loosened
as my father folds his hands, lowers his head.
The rolling thunder on the surface of a nail.
I pick up the cross that seesaws his chest
with each step. The day I lost my faith.
The night my dog ran away and came back sick.
The battery pump of her final breath.
Still wondering if she left alone,
or if my father walked her out of this world.
Still wondering what he used for a leash.
I go further into the trees and find
more fuel. My friends faded on oxy
and percocet. My cousin Josh
buried young in the floodplain.
My brother and the ways I burden him.
Living it over and over each night.
My father walking into every dream.
My fire not bright enough to reveal anything.
Not even his face. Not even the leash.

# COUSIN JOSH ON DOOMSDAY

*Fargo, North Dakota*

It don't matter what you believe. Could be a chunk
of the sun wipin out the grid just as likely
as the Lord Himself snuffin us out one by one
like a bunch of candlewicks. Could be a oil shortage.
Or the souls of the dead come back to reckon.
My buddy Critter figures it'll be the Lake of Fire—
all the flesh dripping off our dicks while we drown
at the same time over and over forever.
But most folks won't tell you what they believe.
My ma, she never broke silence on the issue.
My old man, he says I'm crazy. Says I'm gonna drink
myself to death before anything else gets the chance.
Me, I got my chips pushed in for somethin natural.
A meteor maybe. Or a polar flip. But like I said:
when you're throwin pies, it don't matter much what the flavor is.
It's more folks thinkin like me than you'd think.
And like most of us, I got a bug-in plan for stayin put,
but I also got a bug-out plan for gettin gone.
Not that I'm gonna tell you where I'm goin.
It's high in the mountains—I'll say that much—
but that's all the scat this cat's gonna leave in the sand
for you to track by. Ah, who am I kiddin?
I'll be stuck in this town till God sucks

his last breath. Let me ask you somethin:
You think I'm crazy to have a hundred pounds of Spam
buried in caches? You think I'm crazy to have Critter
shoot me with a .22 so I know what it feels like
to get hit in a bulletproof vest? Well, you know what?
I hope I am crazy. I hope I'm the craziest son of a bitch
you ever met.

# ASKING FOR WORK AT FLATHEAD BIBLE

*All the positions are filled*, the pastor said,
*but you could be a floater.* Meaning
I woke each morning not knowing

and at breakfast a man named Archer
told me what to get busy with. On Monday
I hunched in the kitchen scrubbing beets.

On Tuesday I helped the carpenters
dismantle a barn's gable. The shifts blurred
like faces seen from a carousel pony.

In the laundry I folded linens, in the pottery
I cleaned the kiln, my hands getting nicks
from pulling shingles, stains from applying

glazes, flaky skin from scrubbing
at the scullery's foot-pedal sink.
But none of the wear showed deeply.

Archer called them wishy-washy hands.
*Make up your mind*, he teased, flooding
flapjacks with his homemade syrup.

*Hey, Pastor,* he said, *get a load of these.*
He laid his hands on my hands and turned them
as a father might turn turtles to show his son

the belly patterns. The pastor squinted.
*What am I looking for?* By the time
Archer sent me back to the carpenters

they had the second story down. In the kitchen
the lunch menu changed. The laundry granted
one towel per camper instead of two.

It was easier to adapt than you'd think.
If I had a hammer in my hand, I pulled nails.
If I had a sheet, I found the corners.

# JIM TUCKER LETS ME SLEEP IN HIS TREEHOUSE

*North Platte, Nebraska*

My son built this whole thing: measured
every board, pounded every nail.
Did the trapdoors, windows, knocked out
a wall right where you're standin to fit
the kitchen. Got so he just about lived
in this tree. Did his homework up here,
took meals, ran a cord from the porch
for a heater, even kept a pisspot and a shitter.
His mother fussed, but I warned her:
chain a dog to a leash and all you got
is a beast chewin leather. Let the same dog roam
and it'll circle back home every time,
and that's how it was with Brian.
My boy loved this tree and this tree kept him
busy. Taught him the eye for true,
the eye for level, the eye for inches.
Once you see the world that way
there aint no shakin it. Take these shims here.
That there's four inches, that's three,
that's three and a quarter, that's five, that's five,
that's four, and I can go on like that.
So could Brian before we lost him
to the war. Matter a fact, he had the eye

twice as dialed as mine—could name it
down to an eighth, even a sixteenth.
More than once I called bullshit
and took out the ruler, but my boy
was always right, even when he saw it
from an odd angle. My wife says I got
an inflated sense of my own manhood,
but I tell her I know ten inches
when I see ten inches. And she says,
Jim Tucker, if only you could see
how odd it looks from *this* angle.
Bet you never heard that one before.

# TO THE RAIL COP AT RATHDRUM

You knew you had me for trespassing,
and probably for vandalism, but you weren't sure
how to charge me for the fire still burning
under the train bridge in the railyard you patrolled
nightly, the flames throwing a shiver-glow
on the tagged girders, the rusted tracks, the plastic
unblinking eyeball on the seeable side
of your otherwise unremarkable face.
Arson, you thought, but you knew the word
wouldn't hold up in court. You unbuckled my pack,
hoping for more—dope, or a fingerprinted weapon,
or a scale for weighing and selling. You ran
your flashlight over the bushes, needling the beam
through the barest branches, shocking
the dry leaves with the raw bleached-out colors
of themselves. With your one good eye you caught
my brother's duffle among the torqued shapes
of your shadow-show and realized
I wasn't alone. You cuffed me to a piling.
Tiptoed a search of the firelight's perimeter.
Asked me who it was out there in the dark.
Asked me why he was hiding. Said my silence
couldn't protect him, and only made it worse
for me. You radioed for backup, widened
your circle, your boots glissading the sloped beds

of the railroad tailings. You offered to cut me
a deal for a name. Said the cold truth
was my buddy wouldn't protect me, not once
he was caught, not once he was facing the law.
You'd be surprised, you said. You asked how well
I knew him. Said I should think about that
before I threw myself on the tracks.
Think about that: Who was it out there
in the cold dark hiding? How well did I know him?
As if you needed those questions
half as much as I did, as if you had any stake
in this. And sure enough, after the sky tipped
the dipper into the iron wash of dawn
and my coals smoldered on
in the ritalin moods of the wind, and after failing
to find any ID tucked in the socks
at the bottom of the duffle, you gave up—
drove home, and left me with the day shift.

# EARSHOT

Sure, I was provoked. Eggshell carefully
opened with the tip of a needle-nose.
Black Cat slid down into the yolk.
Lit with a Bic. Thrown so the firecracker
clapped against my ear. Silence tunneling
after, embryo shampooing my hair. Almost
choreographed. More than my brother
hoped for, I know. But believe me when I say
there was no excess in the flat head nail
jeweled through the two-by-four.
No hesitation in my hands, choked up
for accuracy and control. *Shhh*—
I can't hear you anyway. Stop running.
I need to be three feet from your skull.

## FLOOD OF '97

In the flood of '97 everything went to shit.
Somewhere in Canada the Red River clogged
and coated the roads in downtown Fargo
as high as the stop signs. Not much was saved.
Dark water churned for a moment as the river
tipped over, then a stillness filled the basements.
It was the same all over town. The rambler rooftops
looming like islands. Foundations rotting
in the afternoon silence. Everybody camping
in a cousin's backyard, or staying with an uncle
down in Fergus. The old folks at Eventide
had to move to Oak Grove and spent two weeks
sleeping on cots in the brick chapel.
When the ice sheets broke and brown water
flowed up to Hudson Bay, the basements drained
and people opened their own front doors
like strangers. Tiptoed through bedrooms
and ran hands over water-warped walls.
Went in the kitchen and swore the fridge
had been moved. All summer, people found
rusty things they didn't recognize. Things
that must have floated in from other homes.
Fathers walked the silty streets and knocked
on doors, trying to find the rightful owner
of a shovel or a broom. An elderly woman returned

to Eventide and discovered a soggy photograph
on the mildewed carpet in her tiny room.
She peered at the blurry faces and tried to remember
going to Egypt. Wondered who the man could be,
standing beside her at the Sphinx.

## THE RAFT

He baits the hook with an Indian Paintbrush petal,
lets out the line, reels, traps it with his thumb pad.
October. Powder on the peaks. We float on a raft
lashed together with a loose weave of duct tape and rope.
I paddle us forward with a cottonwood branch,
my leg in the water for a rudder, trying to hold us close
to the darkness of the drop-off where the trout go
to stay cool in the afternoons. Later we'll make a fire
and cook our catch with blueberries gathered frozen
from the cirque above the tarn. We'll blow on the coals.
We'll check for tenderness. We'll add ash in place
of salt. But for now I'm watching the sunlight
bounce off the surface and shimmer in the shadow
under my brother's hat. The way he plays the line.
The way he lets it troll behind us. The way the trout
cloud our wake and flick their rainbowed sides.
I'm torquing my leg underwater. I'm turning us back
toward the darkness we've drifted away from.

# COUSIN JOSH ON FAMILY

*Fargo, North Dakota*

You ever had some loose screw try to tell you
your friends is the family you choose?
Well I wouldn't bottle the breath of the minister
that delivered the message. The family you got
is the only family you're gonna get,
take it or leave it. Wanna know what I got?
I got myself sisters. Two of em. But that's all I got
to say about that. That's all I ever knew
to say about my sisters: There's two of em.
I bet I coulda stomached a brother better.
Even when I was a little grommet I wanted
a brother, so I practiced on this pet lizard I had.
He was one of them color-changers that could
change his skin to blend in with whatever's
below him. I named him Tony and took him
around with me. Showed him how to do
whatever I was doin. Talked to him and tried
to explain things. I remember wearin tie-dyed shirts
and puttin Tony on my shoulder so I could
watch him change. One day I had him on the back
of my hand while I was hot-wheelin down the street
and he jumped off and I ran right over him.
What do you say about somethin like that?

Afterwards he was so flat he looked like one of them
outlines of a lizard in a coloring book. No blood
or nothin, like nothin was in him. I'll be damned
if I know what else to say about that.
I don't even know why I told you about it.
Would you believe me if I said I never got over it?
Never got over the fact that when he died
he was the color of my hand?

## OLD CHURCH

Haunted so we didn't follow him
inside. Posing at a broken window
he thumbed the dusty pages, preaching
like our dad. Between passages
he puffed his cheeks and wormed
his fat tongue between forked fingers.
*This is what your mom worships,*
he said. We never told him to stop,
just started chucking rocks from the fence.
First at the shards of stained glass
gummed in the frame like shark teeth.
Then at him. Then at him harder,
his face popping up between our fire
like a self-winding jack-in-the-box.
The bad throw that connected
ricocheted so we didn't see, just heard
our cousin scream. We froze, bracing
for darkness to burst out the door
and roar toward us. But it didn't.
The heavy hinges creaked and Josh
stumbled out holding his lowered head,
pleading for help. At ten years old
I was ready for rage, even death,
even ghosts. But not this: his blond hair
bright with blood, his moan.

## MOORCROFT

You gave me a ride when I was lost
in Wyoming. Took me to your home.
Showed me your gun collection
you had to go shoulder-deep through
the clothes in the closet to reach.
They were old and unloaded, you told me,
and you didn't shoot them anymore,
just oiled them and kept them perfectly
clean. I was careful not to flinch
as I watched the double-barrel raise
and train on my face. The tooth hole
you flashed in the grin after.
The spasm in your hands as you swung
the gun and pointed it at yourself
to show evenness. You told me
about doing five years for murder,
asked if I would've done anything
different, finding a grown man
raping my six-year-old niece.
I wouldn't change it, you said.
I wouldn't take it back. You patted
your heart with your hand.
Family is family, you whispered,
as you brought me clean sheets for my bed.

# LIVING WITH THE ACCIDENT

There was little you couldn't do.
With the purple stump of your thumb
you pinned a pencil against
the knuckle lumps, forming enough grip
to sketch her portrait from memory,
or from the photo you kept hid
in your hatband. You worked the ranches
like before. Rode horses. Knotted
ropes. Shuffled when you dealt.
You let me ball old newsprint
for the fire, but you did everything else.
Gutted the fish. Stuffed the belly
with berries and butter and smoked it
by rotating a willow stick.
And when you folded your hands
to whisper the words over the meal,
nothing folded, but what kind of world
would this be if that mattered?
Your cheeks filled and flickered
as you chewed. The embers bedded down
and the clouds born out of them
twisted through the cottonwoods.
You never told me her name.
*That could jinx it*, you said.
*If I find her again it aint gonna be*

*as a detective.* You could even roll
your own cigarettes, but you couldn't
roll the striker on a Bic.
I flicked it alive for you. Your palms
pulled my hand toward your lips.

# FIRE

There was a time when we didn't know
how to make it. A long time. We ate animals
burned alive in forest fires. Developed a taste
for rare, for medium. Collected embers
and kept them going for generations, firewatchers
in caves danker than prehistory. We roasted
mastodons. Designed skewers, ovens, steam pits.
Invented broiling. Slept with rocks
for the well-held heat. By the time we learned
how to urge smoke from sticks there was nothing
left to do we hadn't already done. We cooked
the same, slept near it the same. The difference
was control. Control kept us going. We smelted
iron blooms in bloomeries. Hammered slag.
Fullered blood gutters to keep the longsword light.
We branded rams—horn, loin, rack, and flank:
Crazy K, Lazy 3, Half-Diamond Flying Double T.
We seared ears off sows to hear if the witches
would scream. They didn't. But the children did
as they crawled away from their napalmed feet.
We made zippos, lifeboats, strike anywheres—
no more bow drill or piston or plow, no socket
fit between the teeth, no calloused hands, no ash
in throats, no 9-volt woke with steel wool—
the flameless, the catalytic, the everlasting.

## POLAROID

A loose flap of skin passes just below
his eye. Bruises ride the bridge of my nose.
The dark ropes of handprints grip
both our necks. Our fresh buzzcuts
lumpy with goose eggs. It's easy to forget
we were trying to kill each other.
Or at least I was. But what I wonder now
is why our father shot the photo before
he bandaged the hole where the nail
went in, stuffed my raw mouth with gauze.
We stand side by side against the garage,
eyes focused just beyond the lens,
each pointing at what we did to the other.

# LILLIAN

*Tarkio, Missouri*

Don't worry about your shoes:
there's nothing you can track
in the door I aint killed before.
Never had a lock till the freeway
came through. Suddenly a gun's missing
from my pickup, tools from the shed.
Go ahead, open the blinds.
Those are apples on the north end,
grapes on the west, tomatoes
out back and corn beyond that.
Goat milk sells as pet food
but people know to drink it.
I gotta laugh to have you crash here—
been trying to get rid of men
altogether. If you were an inch taller
I'd have left you on the side
of the road. Got this double bolt
the same summer they laid
that freeway. Not trying to lock you in,
just making sure the rest stay out.
Don't worry, I never had to kill
nobody. Wanted to kill plenty,
thought about killing even more,

and now with my stuff going missing
in the night—makes me feel crazy,
but the only crazy thing I ever done
was get hitched in Hawaii once.
And Vegas another once.
I figured it was love and I'd worry
about the rest later. Well, the rest
showed up. Now I keep busy
with the plants and animals.

## SHORT BED

Clausen parks the short bed
a hundred yards offshore, locks
the doors and takes the key with him
for no reason he can think of.
Crunches back across the bay to the snow-
sculpted pines on the point, rubbing
his hands together as he walks,
from time to time blowing into them.
Each year in Fargo, men put money
on which day the ice will buckle
under the weight and another truck
will join the sunken junkyard
piled however high on the rust-powdered
lake bottom. The younger men
choose their days based on weather,
average temperatures, and what's supposedly
blowing down from Crookston.
The icefishers gauge their days
by the holes they drill, the relative thickness
they go through. And year after year
Clausen puts his money on May 17th,
and each year he loses, the truck
never lasting past April. He stands
among the great norways
on the shore, the shards of pink bark

flaked off for the routes of squirrels,
misted down onto the snow
like pale blood, nose-blown. He glances
over his shoulder at the truck,
the eye-burning clarity of hard angles
amplified by the drawn sheet
of the frozen lake. He faces the hill
and blinks away the afterimage.

## BETWEEN BOULDERS

Not the last flicker going out, but the wrap
of risen wind on charred wood in the dark.

Not the abandoned copper mine with broken
windows at dawn, but my hand taking a bronze

plumbing pipe to the river. Not the dog's velvet
belly, burst open and spilling wet maggots

on the train tracks, but the tiny pliable femur bone
of a mouse found inside there. We say *I feel*

*so alone*, and we mean we don't know how
to communicate. We say *The dog is dead*

and we mean we aren't listening anymore.
In the growing light I carry my pipe

to the river. I pack it with stolen tobacco.
I hide between boulders. I have no filter,

no friend meeting me. I light it and suck
and my own wind wraps what is inside there.

# COUSIN JOSH GOES OFF ON FOOD STAMPS

*Fargo, North Dakota*

First thing is, I got as much right to get my food stamps
as the next man. Second thing is, what I make of em
is my own Han Solo. State aint got no right
comin around sniffin halfway up my ass, tryin to catch
some little whiff of a goddamn infringement.
If I wanna fetch my breakfast with em, fine,
let a cowboy fry his bacon. If I wanna sell em for cash
or trade em for dope, that's my own Han Solo.
You think I'm gettin rich outta this?
You think I'm puttin some greenbacks away someplace?
Saint me somebody if I'm flush in more than bellybutton lint.
And anyways I'm only sellin em to veterans.
That's the third thing. A lotta vets can't even get
no food stamps, and you mind tellin me why?
You think them boys went off and lost a leg
in Iraq or some other ass crack of the planet
just to come back home to trade me a dime sack
and some percocet? What? So they can hobble
their broke ass down to Deals Only and garner themselves
with nothin but a stone cold bite of somethin to eat?
You tell me. Me, I don't even wanna guess.
And the other thing is, what's the difference

if I got two-three a them food cards?
Who am I hurtin? I'm askin *you*—who am I hurtin?
And I know right off what you're gonna lay on me.
You think I'm reachin in and stealin them tax dollars
right out your own privately owned ass crack.
But the thing is, I aint got your goddamn tax dollars.
Where you think all them sorry-ass one-legged vets
is comin back from? Disneyland?
War aint the Lord's plan, I can tell you that much.
Course, neither is food stamps. Lord's got two hands
and he aint askin for handouts with neither of em.
And you can bet your whole hard-on
he aint givin em away neither. That's why I stopped
prayin. Lord aint givin and Lord aint takin.
Lord's reachin out same way a tree reaches.
Real slow and easy. Sorta callin you in
without callin, cept maybe with the wind.
And your job's as simple as goin to him, cause you're lost
and you know it. And that's the same shake
them vets was expectin to get when they come back
one-legged, but they didn't get that, did they?
No they didn't. Got percocet. And they'll be dosin that shit
till the day they're dead. What's that old sayin?
*Send me home in my casket.* Well, tell you what,
the minute I've gone and dropped off dead
and been laid to rest, you got my god's honest say-so

to bust open my casket and stick a straw
up my ass and suck and see if you find any flavors
that taste just even a little bit like your goddamn tax dollars.

## CLAUSEN'S DOG

We float the rubber lifeboat down the cul-de-sacs,
through the backyards of prefabs and ramblers
where the tops of small trees beckon like oil-
blackened hands. We're looking for animals.
Dogs and cats and other pets left behind
because leaving them behind was the rule
during the evacuation. For hours there's nothing.
Silence and the sculling of a plastic paddle.
The far-off gas station sunken past the pumps.
The hundred-year flood covering everything
three feet deep. When we find Clausen's dog
it's not where we were told to look. Not curled
on his roof, not barking from the glassless window
of his attic. When we find Clausen's dog it's tied
to a cinderblock with a choke-chain leash,
an earflap lapping softly at the surface.
The chain cinches down through loose neck
flesh to visible bone, a minnow hovers
in the eyehole. When we find Clausen's dog
the colorless fur clumps like a stubble of bunchgrass
receding from the furrowed plains of the ribcage.
The bobbing sidemeat nibbled by perch.
Chunks glaumed away by turtles.
When we find Clausen's dog the bone-paws drag
the bottom like lures, jerking forward

on the same wrist-hinge as the living paws
of a sleeping dog, whimpering, trying to run
inside a dream.

## CHECKING FOR TICKS

Before I strip off my clothes I stoke
the fire with oak so the light will last.
I start with my arms, fingers running
the scar carved by the bunk bed's lip.
Chest. Pits. The belly where surgeons
tempered my hernia, my mother rocking
in the emergency wing, praying
without words. Balls. Taint. Inner thigh.
I trace the shin where the bone broke
and growth plate popped out of place,
my brother lifting me to the Taurus
and gunning to Fargo Medical. The heel.
Eight grooves between the toes.
I close my eyes and do the next part
by feel, contorting to reach my back:
the blades, the ribs, the small, the hips.
I scan my scalp where the concussion's lump
still stands, those two nights my dad
stayed awake with me, my head in his lap,
a frozen ham held against the hill
in my hair. Cowlick. Widow's peak.
Finally I find one hooked near my ear.
When I rip it free some of me comes away
with it: a crooked circle of translucent
skin larger than the tick itself.
I lean forward and blow it into flames.

# LYLE CLEARS MY THROAT

*Boone County, Kentucky*

Fair warning: I gotta roll my mother
every half hour or so to curb bedsores,
but I wanna hear this story. Just keep
it down cause she's asleep and I need
the door cracked to hear her heart.
Well, not her heart. The monitor is what
I listen to. It's been a year this June.
I come upstairs and found her on the floor,
drove her to local before they coptered us
to the U. Let me roll her quick and you
can start your travelogue, which I'm dying
to hear. Where we're at now, she can't lift
her own arm, but if you lift it to start with
she can ease it back down real slow,
controlling the speed and choosing
where it lands, you know? They got her
on a food tube and all that, machines
tracking her heart and lungs, the works.
She's basically comatose, but she can shake
her head for no and you'd be surprised
how much power that gives you.

They had her hooked up to this thing—
I don't know what you call it—a shock
treatment kind of thing they hoped
would give her back her speech. But when
they explained all this she shook her head.
Doc said shake once for yes and four for no.
If the math wasn't happening I coulda
called the shots, but you know damn well
that head shook exactly four times.
So they sent us home. Somehow she bosses
me around with that headshake, gets across
every little message. And it's weird,
I used to be as quiet as a mule, but with her
gone mute I feel it's my duty to charm the air.
But enough of me clearing your throat—
I'll shut up so you can tell about your travels,
just let me roll her once more.
Friends ask me how I'm holding up.
That's what they say: How you holding up?
But what they mean to say is this:
How's tending a vegetable that don't grow? Well,
if there's a god and he's listening right now
I'm nothin short of ashamed: this thing beat Jesus
right out of me. But when you lived
what I lived and seen what I seen

happen to who it happened to, there just aint
nothin in it. No order. No holiness.
And don't sit there eyeballing me like maybe
the Lord's breaking earth to sow seeds.
Don't tell me there's a larger purpose.
I won't hear it. I won't listen to another word.

# PRIDE

After pulling a score from the dumpster
behind Krogers I stroll through
sliding doors with egg-caked hands.
The greeter greets me as I pass. I scan
the aisles like a surgeon studying the mint
versions of organs she cuts out
of men. The dented cans of black beans,
undented, would have cost me
ten bucks. The unexpired cartons of cream:
another twenty. I smile at the math.
For the dark roast alone I'd have forked over
forty-seven. For eight uncracked eggs
out of a dozen: about a buck-eleven.
Might as well be money I found.
Might as well be money I made.
By the time I get to the frozen foods
I'm up two hundred. Markdown meats
and I'm up three. In the bathroom
I lock the door behind me and twist
on the tap. As the yellow crust peels
off my hands the mirror clouds over
with steam. I finger the total
where my face used to be.

## NEWS

Whoever you are, they take care of you.
Dean leans over and labors the crank-window,

asking where you need to go. Lillian shows
how to clean and reload. Tucker. The Lees.

Savannah shrunk by cancer. Lyle by diet,
ordering you what he can't eat. Hands that pass

the double cheese and hands that steer the wheel,
a foot floored toward Tennessee, our necks keeping

Hendrix's beat. Each morning another warning
about the darkness out there. Triple murder,

no suspects. Alien abductions in the Palouse.
A family gone missing. A family found,

their organs removed. Each day, against all this
breaking news, another stranger saving you.

## ST. MARY'S MEMORIAL

He wakes to the sound of the television talking,
the blinds drawn, a room that doesn't smell
like his. In the infomercial glow he can see
he's in a hospital gown and his fingers
are missing. He thinks he can feel his thumbs
but when he paws at the gauze he finds
purple stumps. Swollen. Stitched. Last night
when the cops brought him in from the windchill
he was too far gone to know his name
or if he had insurance. Now on the screen
a beautiful woman is selling him
a vacuum. A blender. A new kind
of shampoo. Even before she lets him eat
the orderly begins teaching him how to use
what's left over. What he can hold by pinching
a palm, what he'll have to use his mouth for.
It gets easier, she says, peeling the lid
off a tub of yogurt. The first day is always
the toughest. The man looks down at the blue
slippers on his feet. Stares at the screen
as the woman slices the prices in half. Catches
the orderly's young, educated eyes as she lifts
a plastic spoon for him to bite. Darling,
he says, this aint the first day of anything.

# COUSIN JOSH ON LIGHTHOUSE MISSION

*Fargo, North Dakota*

Don't tell none of the fellas in here, but I'm not
really homeless. I'm just waitin for some shit
to blow over. And truth be told, this aint a bad
little shelter, but I wouldn't even pretend to sleep
if I hadn't landed myself a top bunk. I got my shit
stuffed up in the rafters and my shoes
tied up there too. Some a these guys go lookin
for their size in the night, or at least for somethin
they can trade with. It's anything for a fix
with these crackheads. I don't even take off my kicks
in the shower. Thought I saw some bad bathrooms
in the big house, but at least I made it outta there
without some kinda mushroom growin
on my foot. I did two years on a drug thing,
I don't mind tellin you. Two years up at county
and four years down at the university:
where you think I got my education?
I wouldn't say it too loud among this kinda crowd,
but I'm a republican. Any man with half a head
is a liberal when he's young and a conservative
when he's grown. That's a fact. That's a nature thing.
Speakin of nature, I don't fuck with the food in here.
A couple months back my buddy Critter

found a finger in his pudding cup. A human finger,
and I aint bullshittin. Had a fingernail and everything.
Clipped off below the knuckle. A little tiny one.
Looked like a lady's finger, but it coulda been a child's
just as easy. Before the cops came and took it away,
Critter was fingerprintin dollar bills with the dead
finger, usin the butterscotch like it was ink.
He printed about ten bills, then turned around
and started sellin em for two bucks a pop.
And the craziest thing is, folks was buyin em!
Motherfucker was doublin his luck on each buck,
and I wasn't the only fool to notice. Pretty soon
all the crackheads was takin a extra pudding cup
and tryin to find another finger. Some of these maniacs
is still lookin to this day. Anything for a fix,
like I told you. Anyways, I got mine up in the rafters
if you wanna buy it.

## SOFT HUNTING

Crouching behind a Cosco container
we rattled into Fargo in the dark,
the searchlights raking your face,
warping your nose, the air tubes
hissing in our ears as we whispered
to each other, as you drew the plans
with your finger on my knee.
Or was it me who drew the plans
on your knee? Was it Fargo or Mandan?
Cosco or Hanjin? How would you
describe the train's soft hunting
back and forth on the tracks,
the stutter-stops of all five engines,
the painful groan of a local
lurching forward through the yard?
Could you bring to life the welder
suddenly above us, working
on the girders of a bridge as we passed
underneath? Could you make a stranger
feel the hot sparks cascading—
the way they hovered in the air
like snow, the way they glowed
as we caught them in our oil-
stained hands, the way I brushed them
from your tangled hair. It doesn't matter.

Every version of this story is equally
useless. Because no matter how far
we try to pull away from each other,
no matter how far we ride these coal-
dusted rails over our own Dakotas,
it's always the same old story
with us, the burden of having a brother
coming down on us both like fire.

## THE MARK

Some say fire, some say language.
Some say God made us in his image
on the sixth day. Some say tools,

some religion. Some say whenever
we first dug a hole, marked
a grave—maybe the Neanderthal

family found in northern Spain:
skulls, ribs, jaws, a bowlful of teeth,
a nearly complete spine, a hand,

every digit intact, arranged
below flowstone almost as in life.
Some say art, some crude representation.

Some say cooked caribou
catalyzed the boom in our brains.
Mother, father, child, infant.

Harris lines in the femurs told
how meager their meals were.
Their collarbones gnawed on, sawed

through, hacked at with flint tools,
ribcages crushed with something blunt
to get at the liver and marrow:

if they were buried they were buried
by their murderers. Some say up-
right gaits, opposable thumbs,

three-pound brains. Their skulls
cloven with engraved lithic blades.
The written word. Ritual.

Organs still warm in the middle.
Empathy. A sense of shame. Some say
we're still on the way to human.

# NORTHERN CORN

Traveling alone through Minnesota
as the corn comes in. Steel silos filling
to the brim. Black trees leaning
off the south sides of hills as cold light
falls slantwise against the gristmills.
You have allowed another year to pass.
You have learned very little.
But that little is what you're throwing
in the furnace. That little is stoking the dust-
coals of last year and burning something.
Burning blue. The ninety-year-old father
is bringing his crop in. He climbs
off the combine, checks the engine,
moves an oak branch. He pours
rye whiskey from a thermos and sips
the lidless excess of his private noon.
The size of his hands. The size of one finger.
The flathead prairie of his calloused
thumb pad. He lies awake in the middle
of the night and whispers something
and suddenly loves his son again.
The way excess falls through him.
The way oil runs down the Mississippi River
and remains on the surface and burns.
The father no longer breathing.

The respirator breathing. The father lying
in a hospital bed in a nightgown.
The plastic tubes and machinery.
The whole hospital breathing.
The janitor waxing the vinyl floors
at midnight while life is trying hard
to leave. You must go to your father
while he is still your father.
You must hold him. You must kiss him.
You must listen. You must see the son
in the father and wonder. You must admit
that you wonder. Stand above him
and wonder. Drop his swelled-up hand.
Whisper something. Now unplug the machine.

## CUTTING FOR SIGN

Flat on my back in the sagebrush
as cops cut for sign by the tracks,

snowflakes falling loose and drawled
through their shaky tubes of light.

Wyoming. A fluke September storm.
I've been lying still for so long

snow fills the creases in my coat,
makes moguls on my buttons, drifts

on my brow. Less and less of me
to find. When the flashlights move

down the mainline the flakes turn
to flecks of darkness, visible

against the low, cloud-muffled sky.
My shoes capped with cones

of powder, my outline broken
by crisscrossing sticks. Less and less.

## BUTTE

My brother bolt-cuts a hole through the mesh
over the Family Dollar dumpster in Butte.
I lower myself through. Dull light mumbles
from the car-emptied lot, slumping
on day-old donuts, moldy seed bread,
a bulk bag of oats the rats have chewed through.
I hand up the bread. I hand up the donuts.
I hand up the tub of yogurt someone
bought, opened, tasted, and returned.
I go shoulder-deep through the yolk-crusted bags,
reaching—maybe fruit, maybe meat.
After a while you can name what you feel.
Groping wet shapes with the tips of your fingers.
Lifting them up to your brother.

## COUSIN JOSH ON HIS LIVER

*Fargo, North Dakota*

Ma's always on me about my diet. Always on me
about the cancer and the stomach acid
and the diabetes. So what if my liver gave out?
So what if the doctor says not even a sip?
If a grown man wants to sit back and crack
a cold one that's his own Han Solo. But Ma can't
leave it alone. Can't stop prayin for me.
Says she wants to see her one and only son
in heaven. And I keep tellin her: Ma, you can see me
right now! Feast your eyes! It aint my fault I aint
Christian. I'd be the first man up the believin pole
if there was somethin to believe in.
She sets mantraps every Sunday, but
the truth is, she couldn't drag my ass to church
if I was a sack and she was a dragger.
If the Lord wants me he can come and get me.
I aint hidin. I aint got no sheet over me. Sure, I'll shit
and piss for a few more years, but it's no big secret
I'm a dead man. All Ma wants to wonder is if
I'll be up there dancin when she gets there.
And the thing that knocks my cock around
is how she never doubts her own goddamn grace,
never doubts she'll slide through them pearly gates.

So I'm always teasin her, always askin:
Are the animals up there, Ma? Are the plants?
Are the Neanderthals? I bet the whole planet's
up there. I bet when you get there you don't even
know you're there, cept for all the Neanderthals
walkin around. I bet it's like goin home
to your folks's place years after you moved out—
everything's the same, and everybody's there,
and you're there, and there's that moment
when you first walk in and smell what the house
smells like. You know what I'm talkin about.
Straightaway you know that smell. You know it
better than you know your own goddamn face.
And you know you aint never smelled it
no place else. Not in all these years. Not whiff one.
And the smell rushes at you and fills you up.
And the only thought you can think is how in the dry dive
did I survive all this time without it?

# AFFORDING THE FUNERAL

*for Josh*

Your folks were about to downsize anyway.
The Ford. The riding lawnmower. Letting go
of the furniture was harder. The hope chest
had sailed from Norway with Great-Grandpa Morris
in 1904, but the age and the make made it
liquidable. The trampoline. The jewelry.
There was no need to pay a pastor outside the family.
Uncle Dan did a fine job. Told the story
about the mullet to highlight your stubbornness,
which everyone said afterwards they loved.
The china covered most of the casket. The speedboat
got the headstone. And someone from Odegard
Funeral Home went to Aunt Mary's church,
so they gave us permission to come a day early
and dig the hole. We were told we had to reach
the standard depth, but they were willing
to turn a blind eye while we got there.

## SHOALWATER

Waves grind the shoreline and darken into pools.
Crabs shuffle sideways, lost in the washed-up eelgrass.
Seagulls spit littleneck clams to the rocks
and don't even eat the shattered bodies.
They fly as high as the clouds and wrap talons
in the wind. But this kind of love isn't rare.
When I dream about my brother he disappears
if I look. He wears a bird-bone bracelet,
but I only know this by feel. Even his hair
is something I imagine. His nose occurs solely
as contours. I walk down the beach
and throw stones at the oncoming waves.
This is the best we can do. We leak every time
we are opened. Out just beyond the waves,
love says the same of itself. We can only witness
the implication, only feel for the shape.
Love is a pigeon nestled beside a dead pigeon
at night in the wet corner of a warehouse.
Blackness and the texture of feathers.
The thud of a body surrounded by hollow.
Love is a clamshell's first touch against rock,
whatever tenderness can be found in that contact
before the crack. It's been years since I was last
out on the water. The night sky tightens
like that familiar mouth. Clouds hide their bulk

on the backsides of islands. Each wave is real
the way his body is real. Made of something
not itself. Something bigger. Call it water.
Call it wind. Call it tendon-flexing of the moon.
Each wave lifts as he lifts, crashes as he crashes.
Love exists in the way seagulls hold still
in the wind. The way crabs carry pieces of clam
through the moonlight and vanish sideways into sand.

## MS. RANGE WANTS TO SEE ME IN IT

*Jackson, Tennessee*

Less the Lord crossed my eyes in the night
your shoulders are the twins to my Kyle's.
Let's see how it buttons up. Always was clumsy
with a button, even before my arthritis.
Now twirl around. There they are: those shoulders,
Mississippi-wide. If I didn't know better
I'd tap you on the back and wait for his grin
to turn toward me. Now the pants. I'll look away
while you change. Never did see his body. Bomb
tore him up so good they had to get the name
off his tags. Beyond recognition, they said.
I told those captains I'd know my boy by a glance
at his wrist, just one whiff of one hair off his head.
But men can't sense like that. Or they won't.
Even a father don't dare get that close.
Now the jacket. Kyle hated that decoration,
too showy. And the wool—he used to say
we're southerners: we should know what do
and don't breathe. Here they come again:
those shoulders, each time you turn away from me.

## TAKEN IN

The fear of growing older less than the feeling
of failing to do so. Before first light you grope
down dark hallways in someone else's home,
fingers raking walls for switches. You turn
a valve, strike a match, hover above a burner
and wait for ignition. Whoever owns this kitchen
showed you how to do this, but for a moment
you can't remember where you are, who took
you in. You look around the rooms for clues.
Roughhew of rifles. Couches. Crisco containers.
The tolling black hole of a Peter Pan clock.
A watercolor of Jesus stumbling from his tomb.
You strike another match to eye the faces
on the fridge: not you, not you, not you, not you.

## THE LOW PASSIONS

The Lord came down because God wasn't enough.
He lies on sodden cardboard behind bushes
in the churchyard. Wrapped in faded red. A sleeping bag
he found or traded for. Dark stains like clouds
before a downpour. The stone wall beside him rising,
always rising, the edges of stone going blunt
where the choirboy climbs. He opens his mouth,
but nothing goes in and nothing comes out.
Like the sideshow man who long ago lost
his right testicle to the crossbar of a Huffy.
He peddles the leftover pain. The stitches clipped
a week later by his father, the fiberglass bathtub
running with color, the puffy new scar,
the crooked look of the pitted half-sack.
He tells me you only need one nut, and I want
to believe him. I want to believe he can still
get it up. I want to believe he has daughters, sons,
a grandchild on the way, a wife at home
in a blue apron baking. But why this day-old bread
from the dumpster, this stash of hollow bottles
in the buckthorn, this wrinkled can of Pabst?
The Lord came down because God wasn't enough.
Because the childless man draws the bathwater
and cries. Because the choirboy never sings
as he climbs. Because the bread has all molded

and the mouths are all open. Open to the clotting air.
Homeless, anything helps. Anything. Anything you can
spare. God bless you, God bless you, God bless. God,
Lord God, God God, good God, good Lord very good God.

## YEARS LATER, I GO BACK TO THANK YOU

I walk past the Kwik Trip where you found me
in the dumpster, tunneling for canned food.

Past the VFW where you bought us burgers,
newspaper now taped over the windows.

The bowling alley where you paid for my lane.
The diamond where you coached the Raiders,

now being mowed by a girl, about sixteen,
cap brim curved and lowered, swimsuit

dark beneath her shirt, a spotless Midco
scoreboard lifting above the outfield fence—

Home: nothing, Away: nothing. Your house
is totally different. No garden beds, no covered

porch where I slept. ATVs leak gasoline
in a corrugated shed. When I knock, a stranger

answers the door and holds it half open.
I try to explain. He lowers his eyes and I know

you're dead. He's nothing like you: no leather
hat, no walking cane, no bend in the nose

from the boxing days. But just like you,
he could choose to shake his head, wave goodbye.

He's not my family, not my friend. Doesn't owe me
shit. But just like you, he asks my name,

and where I'm from, and where I'm trying
to get to. And pretty soon, he's inviting me in.

## AFTER FIGHTING

Sometimes my brother and I let go
of rage and snuck in the garage to cut

fistfuls of beef from the chest freezer,
then lay side by side in the pines waiting

for animals to come. We didn't speak.
Hardly even breathed as we played

dead on the rust-colored needles,
the clods of meat cupped loosely

in our upturned palms. And if we waited
long enough, if we let the clods thaw

and seep their blood-deep sweetness,
sometimes a chipmunk slunk up

and nuzzled into our isthmus, crossing
timidly from his hand to mine,

mine to his, chewing. Its hunger
like an invisible line strung between us.

## TO MY COUSIN JOSH WITH NOTHING

I didn't look under the hood the way you would have.
An old Ford hardtop wedged between two trees
in a cornfield as if it was parked there before
the trees took root. The backdoor jimmied open.
The steering wheel in place, but the pedals gone.
I was walking a shortcut to the hospital
because you were dying again. You'd been dying
for so long it was hard to say from what.
Ten years ago it was liquor, which led to diabetes.
Now add cancer. Now pneumonia. The first drops
of rain nickel-and-dimed the windshield but lacked
the body to run the glass. They sat like solo climbers
bivouacked at night on a bald granite face.
I stretched out on what was left of the backseat,
the springs squealing at the pressure points
as if to complain of the various weights of me.
Meanwhile you were adding up to less and less.
Forget about muscle—your skin waxed down
to a windowpane, your limbs thickest at the joints.
And as I lay in that totaled car waiting out the storm,
all I could think about was how you waterskied
at the family cabin years ago, how you slalomed
with a natural's ease, held the towrope one-handed,
carved walls outside the wake, threw eight-foot sprays.
And after a few days in the emergency wing

getting half your liver removed, followed by
that short stint in rehab, I remember the last time
you tried—the same old life vest so oversized
you had to switch it for a kid's one. The easy
bruises on your shins. The towrope assuming
from your hands like a loon before you could lift
above the wake. What happened to that athlete?
That engineer? What slipped from your hands
and skidded across the lake and sank? I couldn't sleep.
The wind picked up. Raindrops veined into each other
and pooled, sluicing down in chutes to the hood.
And honestly Josh, I wish I could say the surgery
failed, or the cancer spread, or the pneumonia found
a foothold. I wish I could tell you I never made it
to the hospital to see you. That in the end it rained all night
and bad luck struck one or the other of the trees
I was under. I wish I could believe the reasons
the preacher gave at the funeral, or the mumbles
of our mothers under the motor-drone on the drive home.
But the truth is, you lived on for years. Thinned
your six-foot-four frame to ninety-five pounds
fully dressed and wet. You didn't lose a fight.
Nothing was after you. You moved up to the family cabin
to avoid paying rent, smoked Camels
with the curtains drawn and the television on,
though you didn't watch it, and one day you were gone.

## LISTENING TO A RAIL IN MANDAN

I've heard it said that you can feel it coming
in the tremor of the tracks, that you can cock
your head and cup an ear to the smooth steel
and sense it coming in vibrations, in rattles,
that you can gather the blaze of friction
as it builds, the heart murmur climbing the pass
through the mountains inside your head.
I stand at the edge of the brake and listen
for far-off signs: whistles, footfalls, gravel
ground under truck tires. I crawl up the grade
to the raised beds and the rails, the bull-run
on the far side of the yard lit by overheads,
each pool of light like a crude betrayal
of the darknesses between. The rails
take parallel trails of light past the sidings,
past the curve at the end of the yard,
past the bottleneck at the Heart River bridge—
two aisles of light like childhood brothers adrift,
like a father's eyes carving the dark land
beside the dark river. The shape of a tree.
The shape of an owl grinding the sky.
I've heard it said that you can feel it coming
from as far off as a mile, the distance erased
in the pump of a vein, in the flicker of overhead lights,
the bull-run laying in its own dust wasted,

the tire tracks zigzagged and stacked
where the rail cop makes fate his listless routine.
I shoulder against a fishplate and lower
my head to the rail. I wait for a chime, a shiver,
some thunder to ride past the overland silence.
I've heard it said that the kingdom of heaven
surrounds us, though we fail to see.
No stars tonight. No fire. No brother by the junkers
awaiting my call. No father walking toward me
on the tar-blackened ties. No dog's eye
catching the searchlights. Not a single sound
fleshing this tank town as the rail begins to shake,
as the train begins to whisper my name.

# NOTES

"Finding Josh" is for Morris Wee

"Great Plains Food Bank" is for Stan Tag

"Leaving Fargo" is for Edgar Kunz

"The Raft" is for Kai Carlson-Wee

"Cousin Josh on Family" is for Mark Jarman

"Lyle Clears My Throat" is for B. H. Fairchild

"Shoalwater" is for Mary Cornish

"Ms. Range Wants to See Me in It" is for Anessa Ibrahim

"The Low Passions" is for Bruce Beasley

## ACKNOWLEDGMENTS

I wish to thank the National Endowment for the Arts, the McKnight Foundation, the Ucross Foundation, the Camargo Foundation, the Frost Place, the Dorothy Sargent Rosenberg Poetry Fund, the Bread Loaf Writers' Conference, the Sewanee Writers' Conference, the Napa Valley Writers' Conference, and Vanderbilt University, with whose support these poems were written.

Grateful acknowledgment is made to the following publications where these poems first appeared, some in earlier versions:

*32 Poems*: "News," "Taken In"

*The Adroit Journal*: "Leaving Fargo"

*AGNI*: "Soft Hunting"

*The Best American Nonrequired Reading 2015*: "Dynamite"

*Best New Poets 2018*: "The Mark"

*Best New Poets 2016*: "Living with the Accident"

*Best New Poets 2014*: "Icefisher"

*Best New Poets 2012*: "Northern Corn"

*Best of the Net 2017*: "McDonald's"

*Blackbird*: "Birdcalls," "Flood of '97," "The Raft"

*Blue Mesa Review*: "McDonald's"

*Bluestem Magazine*: "Between Boulders"

*The Collagist*: "Jim Tucker Lets Me Sleep in His Treehouse"

*Forklift, Ohio*: "Lillian," "Living"

*Gulf Coast*: "Affording the Funeral," "Cousin Josh on His Liver"

*The Iowa Review*: "The Mark"

*The Journal*: "Gathering Firewood on Tinpan"

*Linebreak*: "Clausen's Dog"

*The Los Angeles Review*: "After Fighting," "Old Church"

*Midwestern Gothic*: "Leaving Fargo"

*The Missouri Review*: "Butte," "County 19," "Great Plains Food Bank," "Listening to a Rail in Mandan," "Moorcroft"

*Narrative Magazine*: "Checking for Ticks," "Finding Josh," "Fire," "Lodestar," "Ms. Range Wants to See Me in It"

*New Delta Review*: "Riding the Owl's Eye"

*New England Review*: "Shoalwater"

*New Ohio Review*: "Cousin Josh Goes Off on Food Stamps," "Cousin Josh on Doomsday," "Cousin Josh on Family"

*Ninth Letter*: "Dynamite," "The Low Passions"

*The Paris-American*: "Polaroid"

*The Pinch*: "Icefisher"

*Ploughshares*: "Asking for Work at Flathead Bible"

*Poetry: A Writer's Guide and Anthology*: "Dynamite"

*Poetry Daily* (poems.com): "Dynamite," "Lyle Clears My Throat"

*Poetry International*: "Cutting for Sign"

*Poetry Northwest*: "Primer"

*The Sewanee Review*: "Lyle Clears My Throat"

*The Southern Review*: "Earshot," "Short Bed," "St. Mary's Memorial," "The Muscles in Their Throats," "To My Cousin Josh with Nothing," "To the Rail Cop at Rathdrum"

*The Sun*: "Years Later, I Go Back to Thank You"

*Vinyl Poetry*: "Cousin Josh on Lighthouse Mission"

*Virginia Quarterly Review*: "Pride"

*West Branch*: "Living with the Accident"

"McDonald's" was selected by Ocean Vuong as winner of the 2016 *Blue Mesa Review* Poetry Prize. "Cutting for Sign" was selected by Sherwin Bitsui as winner of the 2017 Poetry International Prize. "The Low Passions" and "Dynamite" were selected by Traci Brimhall as winners of the 2014 *Ninth Letter* Poetry Award. "Riding the Owl's Eye" received the 2014 *New Delta Review* Editors' Choice Prize. "Dynamite," "To the Rail Cop at Rathdrum," and "The Raft" were reprinted in *They Said* (Black Lawrence Press, 2018). "Lillian" was reprinted in *Bad Hombres & Nasty Women* (The Raving Press, 2017). "Birdcalls," "Gathering Firewood on Tinpan," and "Listening to a Rail in Mandan" appeared online in *Poem of the Week*; "Shoalwater" appeared online in *r.kv.r.y. Quarterly*; "Dynamite" appeared online in *Every Day Poems*, *The Lake* (UK), and the National Endowment for the Arts Writers' Corner (arts.gov).

"Riding the Owl's Eye" appeared in the poetry film *Riding the Highline*, codirected by Anders Carlson-Wee and Kai Carlson-Wee. www.ridingthehighline.com

Some of these poems were translated into Chinese and appeared in *Enclave* (China).

Some of these poems appeared in the chapbook *Two-Headed Boy* (Organic Weapon Arts), coauthored with Kai Carlson-Wee.

Some of these poems appeared in the chapbook *Mercy Songs* (Diode Editions), coauthored with Kai Carlson-Wee.

Some of these poems appeared in the chapbook *Dynamite* (Bull City Press).

Thanks to Dorianne Laux, B. H. Fairchild, Claudia Emerson, Ada Limón, Mark Jarman, Kate Daniels, Beth Bachmann, Rick Hilles, Lorrie Moore, Tony Earley, Maurice Manning, Andrew Hudgins, Joan Larkin, A. Van Jordan, Bruce Beasley, Oliver de la Paz, Stan Tag, Mary Cornish, and Dalen Towne—for your teaching and mentoring, which have profoundly blessed me.

Thanks to Jennifer Grotz, Ross White, Laura Kasischke, Patrick Rosal, Traci Brimhall, Adam Latham, Rick Barot, Emily Nemens, Bao Phi, Jessica Faust, Eduardo C. Corral, Tarfia Faizullah, Jamaal May, Gregory Pardlo, sam sax, Patty Paine, George David Clark, Phillip B. Williams, Francine Conley, Matthew Nienow, Paul Tran, Nomi Stone, Emilie Rose, Taneum Bambrick, Tyree Daye, Chloe Honum, Kevin Morgan Watson, Michael Kleber-Diggs, Maudelle Driskell, Patrick Donnelly, Eric Lorberer, Maggie Blake Bailey, Joy Priest, Sandee Gertz, Beth Haverkamp Powers, Christopher P. Locke, Michael Lee, Matt Miller, Joseph Shea, Jim Bodeen, Nathan Barnard, North Campbell, Bretta Ballou, and Steve Ringo—for your friendship and generous support.

Thanks to Hieu Minh Nguyen, Scott Lyon, Michael Bazzett, Leila Chatti, Danez Smith, Matt Rasmussen, Angel Nafis, Michael Torres, Tiana Clark, Gretchen Marquette, Noah Stetzer, Max McDonough, Matthew Wimberley, Javier Zamora, Matthew

Baker, William Brewer, Cate Lycurgus, Brandon Courtney, Malachi Black, Simone Wolff, Alicia Brandewie, and Dan Haney—for your friendship and close readings of these poems.

My deepest thanks to Bryan Schutmaat for the cover image.

My deepest thanks to Mary Austin Speaker for her design.

My deepest thanks to Todd Boss for lighting the torch and making my biggest dream come true.

My deepest thanks to my editor, Jill Bialosky, for believing in my work and giving it the best possible home.

All my gratitude and love to Edgar Kunz.

All my gratitude and love to Anessa Ibrahim.

All my gratitude and love to Mom, Dad, Kai, and Olaf—for everything.

## ABOUT THE AUTHOR

**ANDERS CARLSON-WEE** is the son of two Lutheran pastors. He was a professional rollerblader before he studied wilderness survival and started hopping freight trains to see the country. Staying in the homes of strangers along the way, he has bicycled across the United States twice, hitchhiked to the Yukon and back, and walked on foot across Croatia and Bosnia through the farm villages of the Dinaric Alps. The recipient of fellowships from the National Endowment for the Arts, the McKnight Foundation, the Camargo Foundation, the Frost Place, Bread Loaf, the Sewanee Writers' Conference, and the Napa Valley Writers' Conference, he has published work in *The Nation*, *BuzzFeed*, *The Kenyon Review*, *Ploughshares*, *Tin House*, *Poetry Daily*, *New England Review*, *The Sun*, *Best New Poets*, *Best of the Net*, and *The Best American Nonrequired Reading*. With his brother Kai Carlson-Wee, he is coauthor of two chapbooks and codirector of the award-winning poetry film *Riding the Highline*. His debut chapbook, *Dynamite*, won the Frost Place Chapbook Prize. Anders is the winner of *Ninth Letter*'s Poetry Award, *Blue Mesa Review*'s Poetry Prize, *New Delta Review*'s Editors' Choice Prize, and the 2017 Poetry International Prize. His work has been translated into Chinese. He holds an MFA from Vanderbilt University and lives in Minneapolis.

www.anderscarlsonwee.com